Written by Roberta Brown and Sue Carey
Pictures by Sal Murdocca

SCHOLASTIC INC.
New York Toronto London Auckland Sydney

Printed in the U.S.A.
ISBN 0-590-27555-0
ISBN 0-590-29243-9 (meets NASTA specifications)

17181920 23 0100999897

"One, two, three, four, five, six, seven, eight, nine, ten," Miguel said.

"Ready or not, here I come!"
he called.

He looked in the closet.

Nobody there.

He looked in the closet.

Nobody there.

He went upstairs.

Nobody there.

He looked in the hall.

Nobody there.

He looked in the kitchen.

Nobody there.

He looked on the porch.

Nobody there.

"I give up," he said.

"Here we are!" everyone yelled.